1. Introduction

Why do exclusive arrangements in which a dominant input supplier pays downstream firms not to use a small rival's input cause antitrust concern? Intuitively there is a sense that a "large" supplier can use its size to prevent a competing supplier that is "too small to defend itself" from making sales, even though such sales would be socially efficient. I formalize this intuition by modeling dominance explicitly, and show that if a dominant supplier is large enough and a rival is small enough, then the dominant supplier will pay downstream firms to either completely or partially exclude the small rival, to the detriment of overall welfare.

In the simplest framework the broad intuition requires several pieces. First, input supplier, D, can exclude a rival input supplier, R, from a downstream firm that uses the inputs if D makes a payment to that firm for exclusivity equal to the maximum additional profits that the downstream firm could earn if it used R's input. D can exclude R entirely from the market if D makes such a payment to each downstream firm that purchases inputs.

Second, if D can exclude R entirely from a portion of the market, then D can extract the monopoly rents by setting the monopoly input price in that portion of the market. If D cannot exclude R entirely, then D competes with R, and D can only earn the rents that can be generated in competition.

Third, if the difference between the monopoly rents that D can earn when R is excluded and the competitive rents that D can earn when R is not excluded exceed the sum of the payments D must make to all downstream firms to exclude R, then D has an incentive to exclude R.

This paper identifies conditions under which D has an incentive to exclude R. To do this I formally model dominance as a result of asymmetric demand. Two suppliers sell inputs to downstream firms who make final goods and compete with each other to sell their goods to end users. The dominant supplier's input generates a final good that is preferred by a large majority of end users who will pay a large premium for it. A smaller rival sells an input that generates a final good that is preferred by a small segment of end users who will pay a small premium for it.

1

When there is intense competition between input suppliers, the profit that one down-stream firm can earn from using R's input is bounded by the total premium the end users who prefer R's input will pay. Thus, one condition that contributes to (welfare reducing) exclusion is that the small rival's input generates a small level of premiums in competition. A second condition is that R faces competition from D. Thus, as I will explain below, the premium that end users who prefer the dominant supplier's input will pay must be "large" relative to the rents the small rival could generate to ensure the dominant supplier remains in the market and competes.

Excluding the small rival allows D to charge the monopoly price for his input. If any firm should breach exclusivity then D would lower his price to the competitive level for units sold to end users who prefer R's input. The ability to discriminate in this way allows the dominant supplier to compete away the benefits of any low price the small rival might offer, while maintaining the profits from sales to end users that prefer his own input. This limits the benefit the small rival can bestow on downstream firms from using his input.

While it may initially seem odd to assume an input supplier could price discriminate based on an end user's likelihood of purchasing a rival's product, this is precisely the type of behavior the FTC ascribed to Intel during its investigation of it behavior regarding AMD.

> "These practices [exclusive contracts] severely limited the number of instances in which OEMs [original equipment manufacturers]selling non-Intel-based PCs competed directly against OEMs selling Intel-based PCs, especially in servers and in commercial desktops and notebooks. *When an OEM selling Intel-based PCs competed against OEMs selling AMD-based PCs, Intel often had to sell CPUs at competitive prices. When such competition was eliminated, Intel could sell CPUs at supra-competitive prices.* Consequently, it [Intel] was able simultaneously to charge above-competitive prices and at the same time to exclude its rivals, resulting in both higher prices and fewer choices for consumers."[1]

This indicates that Intel set end user specific prices by offering lower prices to OEMs selling Intel based PCs to end user who were more likely to buy AMD based PC. My model is consistent with this practice.

---

[1] See In the Matter of Intel Corporation (2010) at 48341. Emphasis added.

The intuition above indicates how a dominant supplier can use exclusives to completely exclude sales by the small rival. But, in many instances authorities have challenged so called market share or other loyalty based discounts, under which downstream firms agree to use the dominant supplier's input in a large share of their output, but not exclusively. This allows downstream firms to sell some units using the small rival's inputs. Markets in which exclusionary behavior occurs when a small rival operates and will continue to operate constitute an important set of cases. Many private antitrust actions that challenge exclusive dealing or loyalty discounting are brought by a smaller rival that is already in the market and making sales.[2] Similarly, there are government suits that assail the use of exclusive dealing or loyalty discounts a smaller rival continues to operate profitably.[3]

I extend the intuition from the case in which the dominant supplier excludes a rival completely to the case of near exclusion. So for example, if the supplier pays each downstream firms to use his input in at least 90% of the units they produce then he can monopolize 90% of the market and charge the monopoly price in that 90% to the detriment of social welfare.

The recent literature on exclusive contracts cannot generate this result. In the absence of network effect it can only generate competitive harm from an incumbent monopolist blocking the

---

[2] See e.g. Concord Boat Corp. v. Brunswick Corp.,207 F.3d 1039 (8th. Cir. 2000) in which several boat makers sued stern drive engine manufacturer Brunswick for using market share discounts when selling engines, excluding other engine manufacturers. In AMD v Intel, AMD sued Intel for use of exclusive arrangements with Original Equipment Manufacturers (OEMs). See "Settlement agreement between Advanced Micro Devices and Intel Corporation," (2009). See also Masimo Corp. v. Tyco Health Care Group, L.P., No. CV-02-4770 MRP, 2004 U.S. Dist. LEXIS 26916 (C.D. Cal. June 10, 2004) in which Masimo Corp challenged Tyco's use of bundled discounts, which Masimo alleged foreclosed a significant portion of the pulse oximetry market.

[3] For example, in a recent suit against a dominant battery separator supplier the FTC stated, "Daramic threatened to withhold volumes of separators requested by certain customers to pressure them [customers] to enter exclusive supply agreements with Daramic, and thereby foreclose Microporous from expanding its business with those customers." See, "In the Matter of Polypore International" (2008) paragraph 40. More recently the E.C. found that Intel had among other things used exclusive dealing to reduce competition with AMD. See "Antitrust: Commission imposes fine of €1.06 bn on Intel for abuse of dominant position; orders Intel to cease illegal practices" (2009). The FTC filed a complaint against McCormick spice for making payments to grocery chains as part of agreements that …"restrict[ed] the ability of customers to deal in the products of competing spice suppliers. See "In the matter of McCormick Spice" (2000).

entry of an entrant[4] (or driving a competitor out of the market) leading some to believe that exclusives can only create harm by completely eliminating a competitor.[5] My results show that exclusive or near exclusive arrangements can lower welfare even if the rival remains in the market and is profitable.

The current literature is limited because it relies on two artificial assumptions. First, only the incumbent can offer exclusive contracts. Second, the small rival is an entrant that can be prevented from sinking a fixed cost and entering. My model replaces these assumptions with a formal model of dominance of an input supplier.

My model assumes inelastic market demand, and competing homogeneous downstream manufacturers. This structure has two important properties. First because demand in each segment is perfectly inelastic, each input supplier can extract its full incremental value with linear prices. Consequently extracting uncaptured quasi-rents is not a motivation for exclusivity as it is in earlier literature.[6] This implies that allowing suppliers to use two part tariffs yields the same equilibrium that occurs under linear prices.

Second, manufacturers earn no quasi-rents when competing against other manufacturers using the same input. This eliminates the possibility of "punishment strategies" on the part of the dominant supplier. That is if a manufacturer were earning quasi-rents by using the dominant supplier's inputs, the dominant supplier could threaten not to sell the manufacturer these inputs, or raise the price of these inputs if the manufacturer were not exclusive to the dominant supplier.

---

[4] E.g. Fumagalli and Motta (2006), Simpson and Wickelgren (2007a), Abito and Wright (2008) and earlier, Rasmusen et al. (1991), and Aghion and Bolton (1987). One exception is Doganoglu, Toker & Wright (2010) but this requires both network externalities and multi-homing. There is of course a vast literature on circumstances in which exclusive arrangements can increase social and consumer welfare. See e.g. Lafontaine and Slade (2008).

[5] See e.g. Concord Boat v Brunswick 207 F.3d 1029 (8th Cir. 2001).

[6] Mathewson and Winter (1987) explicitly looked at competition between a large and small input supplier. They showed exclusive contracts could extract downstream quasi-rents that were left uncaptured by linear input prices. Since in my model downstream firms earn no quasi-rents in the non-exclusion equilibrium, my explanation differs from theirs Their analysis is appropriate only where there is little downstream competition.

Eliminating the quasi-rents eliminates such strategies and allows the model to focus on explicit payments in exchange for exclusivity.[7]

Briefly, the contributions of this paper include: i) formally modeling dominance of an input supplier competing against a smaller rival and selling to downstream competitors, thus eliminating the "incumbent/entrant paradigm[8]" ii) showing market share discounts with threshold levels of less than 100%, which allow the small rival to make strictly positive sales, lower welfare[9], iii) showing that the incentive to exclude includes savings from reducing competition in segments in which the small rival would not make sales, but would exert competitive pressure, iv) showing that exclusivity payments need not result in below cost effective prices to lower welfare, v) providing conditions that help determine if increased downstream product differentiation will make exclusion easier or harder, and vi) providing a model in which all pertinent calculations can be shown on a single graph.

Section 2 explains at some length how my results fit in to the most closely related literature. Section 3 formally shows exclusivity and near exclusivity can lower welfare. Section 4 discusses some of the more critical assumptions in the model and a number of policy implications of my results. Section 5 concludes with a discussion of future research.

2. Related Literature

My paper extends the literature on competitive harm from exclusive contracts when downstream buyers are competing firms. The papers closest to mine in this literature are Fumagalli and Motta (2006), Simpson and Wickelgren (2007a), Abito and Wright (2008).[10]

---

[7] In a companion piece, DeGraba (2009), I show that a dominant supplier can use the threat of punishments to induce downstream firms to accept exclusives. One formal difference between payment strategies and punishment strategies is that downstream firms are better off in the game with payment strategies relative to the benchmark game in which exclusives are prohibited. With punishment strategies these firms are worse off under exclusion that in the game in which exclusion is prohibited.

[8] Doganoglu and Wright (2010) models network effect eliminating the need for modeling entry explicitly.

[9] See also Chen and Shaffer, 2010.

[10] This literature reflects the main idea of Bernheim and Whinston (2008) that for exclusives to be welfare reducing they must impose an externality on parties who are not part of the transaction.

These papers trace their origins in two earlier papers, Rasmusen, Ramseyer and Wiley (1991), (RRW-SW) [11] and Aghion and Bolton (1987) (AB), which considered buyers who were end users.[12]

Both AB and RRW-SW considered an incumbent monopolist with an incentive to exclude a potential entrant who had yet to sink a fixed cost to enter the market. In AB an incumbent and an end user customer sign a contract that commits the customer to pay the incumbent a penalty if she buys from the entrant. Therefore, the entrant must compensate the customer for this payment if it enters. If the entrant is only somewhat more efficient than the incumbent, then the entrant is unable to under-price profitably the incumbent and compensate the customer, and so is excluded to the detriment of welfare.

In RRW-SW the entrant must sell to n end user customers to recover its fixed entry cost. If the incumbent signs at least all but $n-2$ customers to exclusive contracts, then the entrant does not sink the fixed cost, allowing the incumbent to charge a monopoly price.

Fumagalli and Motta (2006) replace the end user customers in RRW-SW with competing firms. They argue that if the firms are very differentiated then they behave very similarly to end users in RRW-SW and a coordination failure induced by exclusive contracts can prevent entry by limiting the size of the market to which the entrant can sell. However, they argue that when downstream firms are homogenous Bertrand competitors a single buyer can give the entrant access to the entire market so the coordination failure is eliminated and exclusion is impossible.[13]

Simpson and Wickelgren (2007) largely replace end users in AB with competing downstream retailers who are required to pay expectation damages to the incumbent equal to the incumbent's full lost monopoly rents if they buy from the entrant. This paper is the first to emphasize that competition among homogeneous downstream firms can limit the value that

---

[11] Segal and Whinston (2000) expanded Rasmusen et al.'s results and so are cited as a unit.
[12] Innes and Sexton look at coalitions of buyers that promote entry, but these buyers are end users.
[13] But Wright (2009) shows that the Fumagalli and Motta results are not general, showing that allowing upstream suppliers to use two part tariffs can result in a coordination failure and exclusion when downstream firms are homogeneous Bertrand competitors if the fixed costs are large enough.

downstream firms obtain from buying a low priced input from the entrant, because downstream competition will pass most of this savings on to end users in the form of lower prices. Thus, unlike Fumagalli and Motta they find that if the downstream firms are Bertrand competitors, exclusive contracts (with an expectations payment) can exclude the entrant and lower welfare.

Abito and Wright (2008) rely neither on an Aghion and Bolton-like damages payment nor a coordination failure among downstream firms. They show that with near homogeneous downstream competition, exclusive contracts can prevent entry using only the assumptions that the entrant cannot make exclusive offers and that it must sink a fixed cost to enter. With linear pricing they find that more homogeneity between the two downstream competitors makes exclusion easier as well. When the upstream firms use two part tariffs they always find that entry can be prevented in equilibrium.

My paper extends the progression by replacing the assumptions that the small rival can not make exclusivity offers and its need to sink a cost of entry with a formal model of co-existing competing upstream suppliers where one is dominant due to demand asymmetries. This allows for a model in which exclusionary contracts are used, are harmful and allow the small rival to make strictly positive sales in some cases. It also facilitates a more in depth analysis of the effect of downstream firm differentiation on the likelihood exclusive contracts lower welfare.

An earlier line of the literature exemplified by Mathewson and Winter (1987) (MW) looked explicitly at competition between a large and small supplier when the downstream market consists of exactly a monopolist retailer. In that paper the suppliers set linear prices, and so because of double marginalization, leave some of the rents in the hands of the downstream retailer. The dominant supplier uses exclusive contracts to capture some of these otherwise uncaptured rents.

Having only this tool at his disposal, the dominant supplier offers the retailer an "all or nothing" proposition. When there is a sufficient disparity in the sizes of the upstream competitors and significant substitution between their inputs, exclusive deals by the incumbent occur and result in lower prices and increased in welfare. Increasing the disparity then decreases welfare and might

7

increase prices. As the disparity in demand gets even larger, exclusives can lower welfare and raise prices slightly relative to the no exclusive equilibrium.

The mechanism in MW is completely different from that in this paper. In this paper exclusive contracts prevent input price competition, which downstream competition would pass through to end users (just as Simpson and Wickelgren (2007a), Fumagalli and Motta (2006), and Abito and Wright (2008)). There is no downstream competition in MW so their paper cannot address this issue. MW show exclusive contracts are used to capture quasi-rents that would be uncaptured if exclusives were prohibited. Since in my model no quasi-rents are generated in the non-exclusion equilibrium, the mechanism in MW cannot be related to the results in my paper.

The practical effect of this is that MW is not appropriate for evaluating the effects of exclusive contracts by an input supplier who sells to downstream retailers among which there is significant competition. Thus, MW would have little to say about the use of exclusivity in the Intel case, or *Concord Boat*, where the price of the input played an important role in the ability of downstream firms to compete against each other. However, in a case such as *Standard Fashions v. Magrane-Houston Co*,[14] in which downstream buyers are effectively local monopolists and therefore do not compete, their analysis would be more appropriate.

Finally, MW relies on restricting the dominant firm from using pricing contracts that allow it to extract much of the downstream rents it generates. This subjects their analysis to the criticism that inefficient exclusive contracts are used only because more efficient contracts that don't use exclusivity are artificially ruled out.[15]

My paper is not subject to this criticism. In the benchmark market with no exclusivity, every firm that is a monopolist over some aspect of the final good captures all of the rents associated with that aspect. Thus, allowing two part tariffs would not change the equilibrium results in my paper.

---

[14] See Standard Fashions Co. v. Magrane-Houston Co., 258 U. S. 346 (1922).

[15] O'Brien and Schaffer (1997) shows that allowing two part tariffs results in exclusion equilibria being Pareto dominated by more efficient non-exclusion equilibria in an MW-like model. Some recent papers point out that firms often use simple linear prices. See e.g., Greenlee, Reitman and Sibley (2008) in which buyers are final goods users and Simpson and Wickelgren (2007b) in which buyers are competing downstream firms.

A recent paper that departs from this progression is Ordover and Shaffer (2007). It provides a model in which customers purchase in each of two periods, there are switching costs, and the small competing seller is capital constrained. In this case the unconstrained seller can offer exclusives and with a price that yields a negative profit in the first period to end user customers and the capital constrained seller cannot match this offer. In the second period the switching cost allows the unconstrained firm to charge the monopoly price. My paper offers a different set of conditions that generate exclusive contracts in that I do not need a sales externality across periods nor a capital constraint on the part of the excluded seller to generate my results.

3. Formal Model

Competing downstream manufacturers[16] produce and sell a final good which requires the use of either input, d, sold by a dominant input supplier D, or input r, sold by a small rival supplier, R. Suppliers' marginal cost of supplying the input is zero. Manufacturers convert a unit of the input into a unit of the final good at zero marginal cost. With a slight abuse of notation, $i \in \{D, R\}$ or $\{d, r\}$ indexes both the supplier's name and the supplier's input.

There is a continuum of end users of mass q_c, called the contestable segment, who will pay w_{cr} for an r-based unit of the final good, and $w_d \leq w_{cr}$ for a d-based unit.[17] There is a second continuum of end users of mass $q_n > q_c$, called the non-contestable segment, who will pay w_d for a d-based unit and $w_{nr} < w_d$ for an r-based unit, with w_{nr} "significantly less" than w_d. This formulation captures the notion that D sells a "must have input."[18] That is, a large portion of end

---

[16] Downstream firms could also be thought of as retailers who sell to end users.

[17] The results of this model will still go through if we assume $w_{cr} \leq w_d$. That would be the case in which the dominant supplier is at least as efficient as the rival at serving all customers in the market.

[18] One way to obtain this structure is to assume that there are two attributes over which customers have different value, say productivity and probability of failure. r is more productive than d when r works, but d works for sure while r has some probability of failure, and a replacement r can be obtained with some time lag. There are then two types of end users, those that incur a large cost if r fails (e.g., end users that provide real time services who would be harmed if r failed) and those that would not suffer significantly incur virtually no loss if r failed. The former group would pay significantly more for the security of d and the latter group would pay extra for the additional productivity of r. While it is easiest to think of

users will pay significantly more for a d-based unit than an r-based unit. $s \in \{c, n\}$ indexes the segment. Figure 1 presents a graph of the market demand induced by these preferences.[19]

There are f manufacturers who can use d to produce a final good. $m \leq f$ of these manufacturers can also use r to produce the final good. Manufacturers are indexed by $j \in \{0,...,f\}$.

Supplier i sells his input by setting a manufacturer and segment specific per unit transfer price, t_{ijs}.[20] That is, suppliers can offer a different price for units used in final goods sold to the contestable segment and to the non-contestable segment. (I discuss how this is done institutionally in Section 4.) Given that manufacturers have zero production costs, each manufacturer's marginal cost is equal to the price he pays for the input. He can thus have different marginal costs depending on which end users he serves and which inputs he uses. Manufacturers can price discriminate between segments. Let p_{jsi} be manufacturer j's price for a good to customers in segment s using input i.

Figure 1 – demand for r-based and d-based units

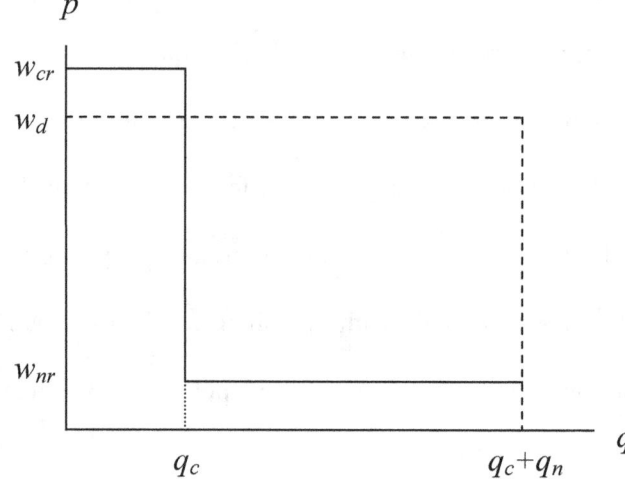

I assume that end user segment is non-contractible, which means that the parties could never prove to a judge the willingness to pay of a given end user. Thus, they can not write a contract that based ex post payments (i.e., exclusivity payments) on the identities of the customer to whom units are sold. However customer specific rebates can be made at the time of a sale to a customer if both D and the manufacturer recognize that they will lose a sale if they don't offer the customer a final good price based on a low input price.

Given this structure I construct the following formal game:

- In stage 1 the suppliers simultaneously offer payments, P_{ij}, to each manufacturer in exchange for exclusivity. Manufacturers state which exclusive offers (if any) they accept.

- In stage 2 suppliers observe who has accepted exclusive offers and set input prices, t_{ijs}.

- In stage 3 manufacturers observe prices, and if they accepted an exclusive offer, announce if they intend to breach.[21]

- In stage 4 both suppliers observe if any manufacturers announce they will breach. If a manufacturer breaches, suppliers can offer lower prices, t_{ijs}, to any manufacturer.[22]

- Manufacturers observe the new prices, and set their final good prices to end users for each segment, p_{jsi}.

- End users make their purchases.

I consider only subgame perfect Nash equilibria. Before presenting the main propositions, I provide an observation and two preliminary lemmas. All proofs are in the appendix.

Observation 1. In the subgame beginning in sage 3 in which no manufacturer has accepted exclusivity, the unique equilibrium continuation has D setting $t_{djc} = 0$, and $t_{djn} = w_d - w_{nr}$, R setting $t_{rjc} = w_{cr}\text{-}w_d$, and $t_{rjn} - 0$ for all j. End users buy r-based units in the c segment at $p_{jcr} = w_{cr} - w_d$ and d based units at $p_{jnr} = w_d - w_{nr}$ in the n segment.

---

[21] Stages 1 and 3 could be collapsed eliminating the need for stage 4. However, the timing I use implies exclusivity does not have to rely on court enforceable contract clauses.

[22] One can think of stage 3 and 4 as modeling a market in which the continuum of end users purchase over time. Then for example D can instantly observe if an end user of measure 0 purchases an r-based unit which would mean a manufacturer breached an exclusivity agreement. He then offers lower prices to non breaching manufacturers so that he can be competitive.

Observation 1 just says that with no exclusive contracts the equilibrium is the competitive equilibrium where each segment has the "usual" Bertrand price. This equilibrium maximizes social surplus.

Lemma 1. If $(w_d - w_{nr})q_n > (w_{cr}q_c + w_{nr}q_n)/f$ then in every subgame perfect continuation in which R offers payments for exclusivity, where the sum of the payments is no greater than $(w_{cr}q_c + w_{nr}q_n)$, (which is the maximum monopoly profit R can generate) not all manufacturers are exclusive to R.

Lemma 1 provides a sufficient condition for D to be "dominant." It says that the incremental value D generates in the non-contestable segment (LHS) has to be larger than the best payments R could make to manufacturers for exclusivity if R were a monopolist (RHS). If D were excluded he would lose this incremental value. If one manufacturer used d, then D would capture this value. He would therefore be willing to share enough of these rents with one manufacturer so that the manufacturer could earn more profits selling d-based units in the non-contestable segment than the payment that the small rival offered for exclusivity.[23]

Lemma 2 now presents the important implication of lemma 1.

Lemma 2. r-based units cannot generate rents in excess of $(w_{cr} - w_d)q_c$ if D competes in the c segment.

Lemma 2 says if just one manufacturer is not exclusive to r in the c segment, then the equilibrium is the competitive Bertrand equilibrium outlined in observation 1. In this equilibrium

---

[23] Some might worry that in a more complex game D's offer of $t_{dj'n}$ might be subject to opportunistic behavior by D in later stages of the game (i.e., different price offers to other manufacturers). This possibility could easily be eliminated by inserting another stage into the game in which once suppliers observe who has accepted exclusivity, a supplier gets to make counter-offers of a payment for exclusivity if all of the manufacturers have agreed to exclusivity with the other supplier. In this case D could just offer manufacturer j' a fixed payment marginally larger than the largest payment R could offer in exchange for exclusivity. Such a payment would not be subject to any potential ex-post pricing opportunism on the part of D.

the highest rent R could generate is the difference between the value of his input and the value of D's input in the contestable segment. That is, competition in the contestable segment will drive R's rents down to r's incremental value relative to d for c segment end users.

The two lemmas together say that even though he can offer exclusive contracts, R cannot monopolize the market by signing up all manufacturers to exclusives. Thus, he will be relegated to fending off D's attempts to monopolize the market, but he has only the difference between his input's value and the dominant supplier's input's value in the contestable segment with which to work. Proposition 1 now states the conditions under which this is not enough.

Proposition 1. If $w_d q_c + w_{nr} q_n > m(w_{cr}-w_d)q_c$ and $(w_d - w_{nr})q_n > (w_{cr}q_c + w_{nr}q_n)/f$, then there exists an equilibrium in which D pays each of the manufacturers $P_{dj} = (w_{cr}-w_d)q_c$ to be d-exclusive and each accepts. R makes no exclusivity offer. D sets $t_{djc} = w_d$ and d-based units are sold to all end users in both segments of the market at a price of w_d.

Further, in off equilibrium path strategies in any subgame in which any manufacturer breaches d-exclusivity, D sets $t_{djc} = 0$ and $t_{djn} = (w_d - w_{nr})$ for all j. In the subgame in which all manufacturers accept an exclusive offer with $P_{dj} = (w_{cr}-w_d)q_c$, R offers one randomly chosen manufacturer, j', $t_{r'js} = 0$ and the remaining m-1 manufacturers $t_{rjs} = w_{cr}-w_d$. In any subgame in which any set of manufacturers accepts a payment, $P_{dj} < (w_{cr}-w_d)q_c$ for d-exclusivity, R offers the manufacturer, j', that accepted the lowest such payment a price $t_{rj'c} = (w_{cr}-w_d) - P_{dj}/q_c$ and the manufacturer breaches d-exclusivity That manufacturer sets $p_{j'cr} = w_{cr}-w_d$. R offers all other manufacturers $t_{r\text{-}j'c} = (w_{cr}-w_d)$.

This equilibrium is strategy is unique.[24]

_____

[24] Since off equilibrium strategy involves choosing a manufacturer at random, there are multiple ex post outcomes if one considers each possible random realization of the selection process as a different equilibrium.

The main intuition behind proposition 1 is that (when the second condition holds) R cannot induce all of the manufacturers to be exclusive to himself because D can always offer one manufacturer some of his incremental value from the non-contestable segment (which D would lose if all manufacturers were exclusive to R) to forgo exclusivity to R. Thus, D will always compete in both segments.

If R and D compete, then R earns only his input's incremental value in the contestable segment and D earns only his input's incremental value in the non-contestable segment. If D excludes R, then D earns the monopoly profits from both segments. If the monopoly profits D could extract from the contestable segment plus the increased profit he could obtain from the non-contestable segment by excluding R is larger than R's incremental value in the non-contestable segment times m, the number of manufacturers that can use r, then D pays each manufacturer for exclusivity, making D a monopolist in the entire market.

Figure 2 – demand for r-based and d-based units

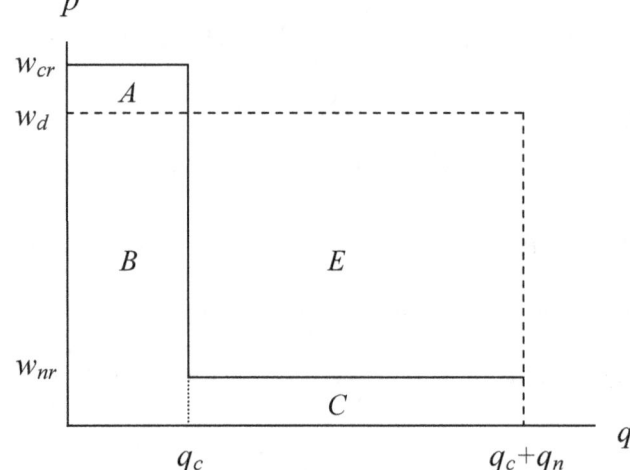

The conditions of proposition 1 have graphical interpretations. In Figure 2 above A is the incremental value R generates in the contestable segment, B is the rent D could extract from the contestable segment if he could monopolize it, E is the incremental value D generates in the non-contestable segment and C is the value R generates in the non-contestable segment and represents

14

the addition profit D would earn in the non-contestable segment if R were excluded. The first condition of proposition 1 says that $B+C > mA$. The second condition says that $E > (A+B+C)/f$.

The first condition highlights the two benefits that the dominant supplier receives from excluding the rival. First, excluding the rival allows the dominant supplier to sell units in the contestable segment at the monopoly price when he would have sold no units in that segment without exclusivity. Second, excluding the rival eliminates price competition in the non-contestable segment, and allows the dominant supplier to charge a higher transfer price, w_d, rather than $(w_d - w_{nr})$ which would occur without exclusivity. Even though he is less efficient in the non-contestable segment, the small rival imposes some competitive pressure on prices in the absence of exclusivity. The exclusive contracts eliminated this competitive effect. This result is not in the current literature because those papers model only one market segment.

The second condition says that the dominant input must generate more rents in the non-contestable segment than one manufacturer must be paid to induce him not to be exclusive to R.

Exclusivity lowers social surplus relative to the competitive benchmark equilibrium (Observation 1) because it allows the less efficient supplier to serve the contestable segment. Consumer surplus is also lower because the exclusivity causes higher final goods prices in both segments. In this simple model the higher price does not lead to a reduction in social surplus because both segments have inelastic demand.[25]

Two intuitive comparative statics results are that (holding all other parameters constant) reducing $w_{cr} - w_d$, or reducing q_c reduces the dominant supplier's cost of excluding the rival. When $w_{cr} = w_d$, D can exclude R by offering a payment of 0 since R has no rents to offer a manufacturer for breaching exclusivity. Note the exclusivity would still make end users uniformly worse off relative to the benchmark in which only linear prices are allowed. This same

---

[25] A simple modification can easily generate the traditional deadweight loss from monopoly pricing. Assume that suppliers and manufacturers can distinguish between segments but cannot tell high from the low willingness to pay end users within the segment. Assume that in segment s a mass of customers ε_s will pay $w_{d\varepsilon s} < w_d$ for a d-based unit where $(w_d - w_{d\varepsilon s})q_s > 2w_d\varepsilon_s$. D prices his input at w_d under this condition pricing lower willingness to pay end users out of the market.

result would hold of course if $w_{cr} < w_d$. This would be the case in which the dominant supplier was more efficient than the rival at serving all customers. Here customers would be worse off from the use of exclusives to exclude a less efficient rival.

Lowering m also reduces the cost of excluding the rival. m close to 1 can be interpreted as there being very few firms that provide complementary products for a small rival and the dominant supplier can exclude the rival by "poisoning the ecosystem," i.e., buying off the few firms that provide complements to the rival.

A third less intuitive result is that increasing w_{nr} increases the parameters for which exclusion occurs when the second condition of proposition 2 is not binding. This is because a higher w_{nr} means more competition in the non-contestable segment, which means lower profits for the dominant supplier if R is not excluded.[26]

In the formulation above R makes no positive sales even though he is "in the market." I now extend the model by assuming that a portion of the contestable segment q_z is willing to pay $w_{zr} > w_{cr}$ for an r-based unit. Figure 3 below shows the resulting demand curve. The game proceeds as in section 4, with the addition that D can offer a "loyalty" payment to a manufacturer for using d in at least a specified percentage of his sales that is less than 100%.[27]

---

[26] Increasing w_{nr} tightens the second condition. However, the first condition would be the binding constraint for a large dominant supplier that generates enough rents to induce one manufacturer to be exclusive.
[27] Allowing R to also offer market share discounts raises the potential for collusion between the suppliers. This is beyond the scope of this paper and is considered in DeGraba (2009).

Figure 3 – demand for *r*-based and *d*-based units

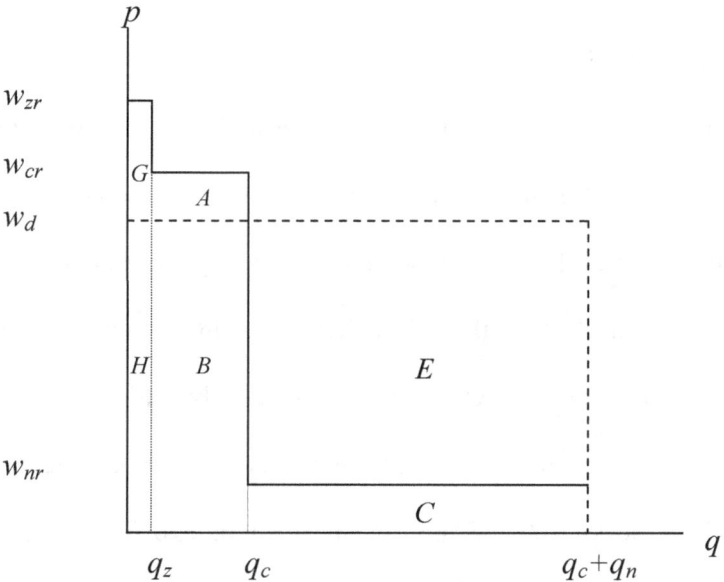

Proposition 2. If $m(w_{zr} - w_d) > w_d$ and $w_d(q_c - q_z) + w_{nr}q_n > m(w_{cr} - w_d)(q_c - q_z)$ then there exists an equilibrium in which the dominant supplier offers each of the *m* manufacturer a payment if his purchases of *r* as a fraction of total input purchases do not exceed $(q_z/m)/(q_z/m + (q_c - q_z)/f + q_n/f)$. Further the payment to each equals $(q_c - q_z)(w_{cr} - w_d)$.

Proposition 2 says that if there are end users with sufficiently high willingness to pay for an *r*-based unit, it is more profitable for *D* to allow them to be served by *r*-based units than to exclude *r* completely. In Figure 3 this says if $mG > H$, then *D* is better off paying mA and extracting *B* than paying $m(G+A)$ and extracting $H+B$. By choosing a market share discount in which the share is equal to one minus the share of the entire market that the high willingness to pay end users constitute, *D* ensures that only those high willingness to pay end users are served by *r*-based units.

The social surplus of the competitive equilibrium is higher than the surplus of the market share discount equilibrium, which is higher than the surplus of the exclusive contract equilibrium. The competitive equilibrium is efficient since *r*-based units serve the contestable segment. In the market share discount equilibrium $q_c - q_z$ end users are served by *d*-based units, which is inefficient. In the exclusive equilibrium all q_c end users in the contestable segment are served by *d*-based units.

4. Discussion

4.1 Model assumptions

Price discrimination

An important feature of the model is D's ability to price discriminate across segments. This allows him to compete away the benefits of lower input prices from R in the contestable segment if manufacturers were to breach exclusivity, while maintaining high prices in the non-contestable segment. As noted in the introduction, the FTC believed that Intel's ability to sell CPUs at low prices when facing competition from AMD and simultaneously at high prices when not facing competition was crucial to the competitive harm from exclusionary arrangements.[28]

In its complaint against Intel the New York State Attorney General explained in some detail how this could be accomplished institutionally.[29] The complaint alleges that when OEMs were responding to requests for proposals (RFPs) from large customers, Intel would work closely with the OEM and collected information on the RFP including whether a non-Intel based PC was being offered by another bidder. If there were, then Intel would issue a discount to the OEM that it believed would be large enough to win the bid. If there were no non-Intel PCs being offered then Intel would not issue a discount. This explanation suggests that exclusives are more likely to be problematic when end users are large customers that ultimately receive a customer specific price (such as the result of an RFP process) rather than say retail customers for which one price applies to many buyers.[30]

---

[28] See quote from FTC Aid to Public Comment in this paper's introduction.

[29] See "State of New York ..." (2009) paragraphs 120-125. This also assumes arbitrage is not possible. In this case since Intel knew the details of the bid process it knew how many units the OEM would purchase as a result of each bid, and give the discount only for those units. Thus, an OEM could not purchase "extra units" for arbitrage purposes. In other settings there may be other ways a dominant supplier could limit arbitrage. For example he might not honor warranties on arbitraged units. Arbitrage might be naturally prevented if the contestable and non-contestable markets are geographically separate, and transport is costly, or if contestable end users require different attributes in the input than non-contestable end users.

[30] The customer could be a competitive retail seller that was large enough to have an RFP. Here Intel might work with an OEM selling to the retailer, or it might pay the retailer directly not to sell non-Intel based PCs.

Exogenously fixed number of manufacturers

I have exogenously fixed f and m in this model. Because I have assumed homogeneous Bertrand competition and 0 fixed costs, something in the model must prevent infinitely many manufacturers from entering the market in response to the dominant supplier's payments. Fixing f and m exogenously would be consistent with a number of potential market characteristics including i) that there are only finitely many entrepreneurs with the ability to produce the final good, ii) it takes several years of successful production to develop a reputation that allows a manufacturer to make a significant volume of sales, iii) there is a long lead time for a new firm to gather the resources and expertise to begin production or iv) the existence of the current manufacturers is a product of a sunk cost in the past that was paid for at a time when the industry was not so homogeneous. Thus, these "legacy" manufacturers remain in the market, but no new manufacturers have an incentive to enter.

These characteristics indicate that homogeneity in the final good does not imply homogeneity across the universe of possible downstream manufacturers. The theory requires that there be a sufficiently small number of manufacturers that can be "bought off" for exclusives to cause harm. This is consistent with the law suits cited in the introduction, which typically accuse the dominant supplier of engaging in such behavior with respect to the largest downstream manufacturers, but not fringe manufacturers, which no one would expect to expand significantly as a result of a low input price from the rival.[31]

Inelastic demand

The lack of demand elasticity or the discontinuous nature of willingness to pay for r-based units has no substantive effect on the results. For example, if we were to replace the willingness to pay for the r-based good with a linear function between the points $(0, w_{cr})$ and $(q_n +$

---

[31] Applying this to the cases in footnotes 2 and 3, these assumptions say that the slotting allowances paid by McCormick were not sufficient to induce a new grocery chain to enter. In the case of Intel, no one would expect that an OEM like eMachines would instantly be able to provide the global availability and client support necessary to compete significantly for multinational business end users.

q_c, w_{nr}) and allow the suppliers to make end-user by end-user price reductions, one would get a benchmark model in which each supplier extracted his incremental value from each customer. This price discrimination is more consistent with end users being large enough to have their own individual bidding process for the final good and the suppliers offering customer specific input prices. When exclusives are allowed, the dominant supplier is able to exclude the rival and charge the monopoly input price.

One important feature of this assumption is that in the benchmark model the manufacturers earn no quasi-rents. This is important for two reasons. First as noted in section 2 this distinguishes my model from that of Mathewson and Winter (1987) as that paper explains how exclusivity is used entirely to capture such rents.

Second, the potential for quasi-rents creates a complicating issue when considering exclusion. If manufacturers earned quasi-rents from sales in the non-contestable segment (presumably to cover a strictly fixed cost of operating) the dominant supplier would be an essential input in earning these quasi-rents. This would allow for a larger set of potentially observable behavior by the dominant supplier including threatening to raise the transfer price (or restrict the quantity) of inputs sold to a breaching manufacturer, thereby "punishing" him by reducing his quasi-rents in the non-contestable segment if the manufacturer used the rival's input in the contestable segment.[32] Such a punishment strategies has (at least) one testable implication that is different from my model. In my model manufacturers are better off under the exclusivity

---

[32] Since the literature does not formally model two segments, this issue is not considered. A complication arises because threatening to withhold inputs from a manufacturer would likely lower the dominant supplier's profits as well. Thus, the supplier might be unwilling to carry out the threat if a manufacturer breached exclusivity. To solve this subgame perfection problem one would either need to develop a reputation model, in which the dominant supplier established a reputation for punishing manufacturers that breached exclusivity, or present a model in which the dominant supplier allows the manufacturers to retain quasi-rents by offering a below short run profit maximizing transfer price in exchange for exclusivity. In this case end users would benefit from the lower input price. Such a model would have to show that the end users benefits from the lower price are smaller than the benefits they would receive from the competition from the small rival if exclusivity were not allowed. DeGraba (2009) considers these issues.

arrangement because they receive a payment they would not receive in the benchmark equilibrium. In a punishment model manufacturers would not be better off under exclusivity.

Other assumptions leading to positive sales by R

Proposition 2 presents a model in which all manufacturers reach near exclusive arrangements with D. It cannot explain a pattern in which the largest manufacturers reach exclusive arrangements and the rival makes sales through smaller manufacturers. To obtain such a result one could extend the model of proposition 1 to assume that there is a low quality version of the final good produced by some manufacturers who do not produce the high quality good,[33] and that a group of customers have a very low willingness to pay for this final good and are not willing to pay any extra for the higher quality version. Assume also that these customers have a higher willingness to pay for R's good than for D's. For example their willingness to pay for an r-based good is $w_{nr} - g$ and their willingness to pay for a d-based good is $w_d - g$ respectively. Clearly for g close to w_d, the first condition of proposition 1 would fail and it would not be profitable for D to pay these manufacturers for exclusivity. R would sell to these manufacturers and they would outbid any manufacturer that was exclusive to D for the "low end" end users. Thus, R would make sales in this low end of the market.

4.2 Public Policy Implications

Price cost tests

A number of commenters have proposed that loyalty arrangements be subject to a price cost test.[34] The test divides the fixed loyalty payment made by a supplier to a manufacturer by the incremental units of the input sold as a result of the loyalty arrangement to obtain an effective discount for these units. It then subtracts this discount from the observed wholesale price of the

---

[33] For example, suppose the final good is PCs and some manufacturers have invested in the ability to design and maintain networks while others have not, and that there are customers that have no need for such networking services.
[34] See e.g., European Commission 2008 page 11, and Economides (2009) page 273.

units to obtain an effective price. The loyalty payment is considered potentially anticompetitive if and only if this effective price is less than the incremental cost of producing these units.

My model shows this test is too restrictive. While there are parameters for which the effective price is less than marginal cost and results in welfare reducing exclusion, there are also conditions under which the effective price is above marginal cost, but loyalty payments still result in a welfare loss and a reduction in consumer surplus relative to the competitive equilibrium. This occurs if $w_d q_c > m(w_{cr} - w_d)q_c$ (which in figure 2 is equivalent to $B > mA$). This implies $w_d - m(w_{cr} - w_d) > 0$. w_d is the observed wholesale price, $m(w_{cr} - w_d)$ is the effective discount per unit sold in the contestable segment and 0 is the marginal cost of production. The price cost test therefore would not find this loyalty payment to be anticompetitive, even though it leads to inefficient exclusion.

The intuition behind this result is that the simple price cost test is incomplete because it implicitly assumes that if an equally efficient rival offered a price just below the effective price, the downstream manufacturer would purchase from the rival at that price. That assumption is unwarranted. If a manufacturer purchased from the rival at a slightly lower price, breaching exclusivity, then the dominant supplier would lower his transfer price, and the resulting competition would lower the price of the final good reducing the profits that the manufacturer would earn by using the rival's input eliminating the incentive for the manufacturer to purchase from the rival. Thus, in this setting the rival cannot make any sales by slightly undercutting the dominant firm's effective price. So the price cost test can be invalid because it mistakenly subtracts the effective discount from the observed wholesale price rather than from the lower wholesale price that would prevail in the event of breach.

Vertical integration as a counterstrategy

This model also implies that the small rival cannot circumvent exclusivity by integrating forward into the downstream market by merging with one of the manufacturers that can use r. In equilibrium the dominant supplier pays each of those downstream manufacturers the incremental value of the small rival's input, which means the small rival would have to pay this amount to the manufacturer's stockholders to induce them to merge. Since the payment is not enough to compensate the manufacturer's stockholders to breech exclusivity as an independent manufacturer, it would not be enough to induce them to cede ownership to the rival instead of accepting an exclusivity payment. Thus, not only can exclusivity payments prevent sales contracts between the small rival and manufacturers, they can also prevent mergers or joint ventures between such parties.

Long term contracts

My results also suggests that exclusive arrangements do not need to be part of long term contracts to be exclusionary. Two features of the model suggest that contract duration is not an element of the equilibrium First the equilibrium does not require any player to commit to a strategy choice that he would prefer not to play when it came time to play. Thus, there is no interpretation in which any player has made a long term commitment. Second, my model does not require agreements to stretch over a period during which a small rival could enter, which often distinguishes short run from long run.

The effect of downstream differentiation

Simpson and Wickelgren (2007a) and Abito and Wright (2008) argue that differentiation among downstream competitors makes exclusion more difficult. I show that this is not a general result. It is simple to introduce a form of differentiation among manufacturers into proposition 1 that makes exclusion easier. Suppose that for each end user in the contestable segment a fraction λ of manufacturers are perfect substitutes, while the other $(1-\lambda)$ are unacceptable, and that which manufacturers are substitutes for a given end user is uniformly distributed across end users.[35] Under this assumption (and continuing the assumption that the dominant supplier can lower prices selectively to customers that are considering a product with a rival's input) the dominant

---

[35] Let customers and manufacturers be uniformly distributed around a Hotelling Circle of circumference 1. Each customer can travel 1/3 in either direction for free, but can go no further. Then $(\lambda=)$ 2/3 of the manufacturers would be perfect substitutes and the other 1/3 would not be considered. One could imagine customers who only will deal with manufacturers with whom they had a positive previous experience. Different customers could have different sets of manufacturers with which they had good experiences.

supplier would only have to pay each manufacturer λA instead of A to be exclusive, lowering the cost of exclusion and increasing the set of parameters for which exclusion is possible.

Differentiation can have two effects on manufacturers. First it can soften price competition among manufacturers. This increases the benefits from a rival's low input price that downstream manufacturers would keep, which makes paying for exclusion more expensive to the dominant supplier. This is the effect that dominates in the Simpson and Wickelgren, and Abito and Wright papers. A second effect is that differentiation limits the size of the market any one manufacturer could serve, limiting the potential profits he could earn by breaching exclusivity. This limits the payment the dominant supplier must make to induce exclusivity. The extension outlined above has only this second effect and so reduces D's cost of inducing exclusivity.

5. Conclusion

The recent literature has modeled exclusion in the context of a potential entrant who is more efficient than a monopolist incumbent across the entire market. The incumbent excludes when the entrant is prevented from making exclusive offers. By contrast I present a model in which a small rival, who is already in the market, is more efficient at serving only a small segment of the market. If the dominant supplier has sufficiently large demand from the segment of the market that he serves more efficiently, then he can use exclusive or other loyalty arrangements to exclude the smaller rival. Such exclusivity reduces social and consumer surplus.

The contributions of this model include i) formally modeling dominance of an input supplier competing against a smaller rival and selling to downstream competitors ii) showing conditions under which a dominant supplier has to be sufficiently large to use exclusive contracts to exclude and lower welfare, ii) showing that a dominant supplier's use of market share discounts with threshold levels of less than 100% lowers welfare, even though the rival sells positive amounts of its inputs, iii) showing formally that the so called price cost tests will fail to detect conditions under which exclusion lowers welfare, iv) showing that the incentive to exclude includes savings from reducing competition in a market segment in which the small rival would not make sales, but would exert competitive pressure, and v) providing some conditions that help determine if increased product differentiation will make exclusion easier or harder.

.

Appendix

Proof Observation 1

Since both suppliers can price discriminate in the two segments and marginal costs are constant, the prices in the two segments are independent. Consider first segment n. For any set of transfer price offers define $\delta_{ijn} \equiv w_{in} - t_{ijn}$ for $i \in \{d, r\}$ and $j \in \{1, 2, \ldots f\}$.[36] Let Δ denote the set of all δ_{ijn}. For any manufacturer j' receiving an offer from supplier i' let $\Delta^{-j'i'n}$ be the set Δ excluding the difference associated with offer $t_{i'j'n}$. Finally let $\delta_{ijn}*$ denote the max of Δ, and $\delta_{ijn}^{-i'j'n}*$ denote the max of $\Delta^{-j'i'n}$. For any set of transfer prices only the manufacturer(s) for which δ_{ijn} is a maximum of Δ can make sales in equilibrium using the input i for which δ_{ijn} is the max of Δ. This is because δ_{ijn} is the maximum surplus manufacturer j using input i can offer an end user without pricing below cost. The subgame perfect $p_{jni} = w_{in} - \delta_{ijn}^{-i'j'n}*$. Suppose there were some equilibrium price $p_{jni}' > w_{in} - \delta_{ijn}^{-i'j'n}*$. Then the manufacturer with the offer associated with $\delta_{ijn}^{-i'j'n}*$ could profitably offer a price that offered customers marginally more surplus than p_{jni}' and sell all the units.

Similarly, if $p_{jni}' < w_{in} - \delta_{ijn}^{-i'j'n}*$ then the manufacturer could marginally raise his price and offer customers more surplus than $\delta_{ijn}*^-$ which no other manufacturer could match if this manufacturer were the only manufacturer receiving a transfer price yielding $\delta_{ijn}*$. If more than one manufacturer had a transfer price that yielded $\delta_{ijn}*$ then $p_{jni}' < w_{in} - \delta_{ijn}^{-i'j'n}*$ implies $p_{jni}' < w_{in} - \delta_{ijn}*$ which implies a price below marginal cost and a negative payoff.

In any equilibrium continuation R sells no units. Consider any price configuration in which R sold positive units to a manufacturer. D could always set a price to that manufacturer marginally above R's price and that manufacturer would be better off purchasing from D. Thus R must earn 0 in this segment.

---

[36] Where I write w_d as w_{dn} for notional consistency and note that for the m-f manufacturers that can not use input r there is no t offer

In any equilibrium continuation prices must be such that if R offered 0 to all manufacturers, he would sell no units. If there were prices such that R could sell positive units at a price of 0 then there is some arbitrarily small positive price at which he could sell positive units and earn a positive payoff.[37] I can therefore limit the analysis to price configurations in which R offers at least one manufacturer a transfer price of 0. In this case D's optimal price is to set $t_{djn} = w_d - w_{nr}$ to at least two manufacturers and a price no lower than $w_d - w_{nr}$ to the remaining manufacturers.

The proof for segment c is identical in structure except of course R sells all the inputs into this segment. $\hspace{5cm} QED$

Proof of Lemma 1

R cannot profitably pay more than a total of $w_{cr}q_c + w_{nr}q_n$ to the f manufacturers for exclusivity since his monopoly profits are capped at $w_{cr}q_c + w_{nr}q_n$. Dividing this among f manufacturers means that (at least) one manufacturer must receive no more than $(w_{cr}q_c + w_{nr}q_n)/f$ for being exclusive to R. If all manufacturers were to accept exclusivity to R then D would earn 0. D could always offer one manufacturer, j', receiving no more than $(w_{cr}q_c + w_{nr}q_n)/f$ a transfer price $t_{dj'n}$ such that $[w_d - w_{nr} - t_{dj'n}]q_n = (w_{cr}q_c + w_{nr}q_n)/f$, and $t_{dj'c} = 0$ and offer a price to no other manufacturer.

Manufacturer j' would breach exclusivity with R. R would then set $t_{rjn} = 0$ and D would make no other offers to manufacturers. Given that price, j' would set $p_{j'nd} = w_d - w_{nr}$ and earn $(w_{cr}q_c + w_{nr}q_n)/f$. D would earn $t_{dj'n}q_n$. This is the most D could earn conditional on j' earning $(w_{cr}q_c + w_{nr}q_n)/f$. Further conditional on D offering $t_{dj'n}$ to j', D cannot earn greater revenue by offering any other manufacturer(s) any other price.

---

[37] Recall that indifferent consumers purchase from the seller whose price is above marginal cost and if all manufacturers set marginal cost prices they purchase from those manufacturers who purchased from a supplier whose price is above marginal cost.

Thus, the continuation after all manufacturers accept exclusivity to R (where the sum of the payments does not exceed $(w_{cr}q_c + w_{nr}q_n)$) will have one manufacturer breaching exclusivity and earning a profit selling d-based units equal to the maximum payment R could offer him for exclusivity.

Proof of Lemma 2

Suppose that D sets $t_{djc} = 0$ for at least one manufacturer. Then, R's best response is to set $t_{rjc} = w_{cr} - w_d$, and D's best response to that is $t_{djc} = 0$. The equilibrium of this subgame is for manufacturers to set $p_{jcd} = 0$ and $p_{jcr} = w_{cr} - w_d$ resulting in total segment sales of $(w_{cr} - w_d)q_c$.

There is no equilibrium in which R sells positive units at any $t_{rjc} > w_{cr} - w_d$ for all j. If R set $t_{rjc}' > w_{cr} - w_d$ for all j, then D could set $t_{djc} > 0$ by an arbitrarily small amount and make positive profits while R earned 0 in the c segment. If R set $t_{rjc} > w_{cr} - w_d$ for some manufacturers and $t_{rjc} = w_{cr} - w_d$ for the rest, then only those manufacturers receiving $t_{rjc} = w_{cr} - w_d$ would make sales in equilibrium. $\hspace{2cm}$ *QED*

Proof of Proposition 1

In the proposed equilibrium each manufacturer earns a payoff of $(w_{cr}-w_d)q_c$. D receives a payoff of $w_d q_c + w_d q_n - m(w_{cr}-w_d)q_c$. R earns a payoff of zero as do all end users.

Suppose one manufacturer deviated by breaching his exclusive contract in response to a price offer between 0 and $w_{cr}-w_d$ from R. Then in the proposed equilibrium's continuation D would offer $t_{djc} = 0$ to manufacturers not R-exclusive and R would still sell at the price that induced the breach. The equilibrium p_{jcr} would equal $w_{cr}-w_d$ and p_{jcd} would equal 0. The manufacturer that sold the r-based good could not earn more than $(w_{cr}-w_d)q_c$, so he could not profit by breaching. R could not profit by offering a price less than 0 to induce a breach. Thus, there is no deviation involving a breach that could make the deviating manufacturer and R jointly better off.

If one manufacturer deviated by simply refusing to accept an exclusive offer, then the only continuation would be for R to set $t_{rjc} = w_{cr}-w_d$ to the non-exclusive manufacturer and for D to set

$t_{djc} = 0$ for any unit sold by a D-exclusive manufacturer to the contestable segment. In the continuation equilibrium the manufacturer would earn a payoff of 0, which is less than the $(w_{cr}-w_d)q_c$ he would earn accepting exclusivity.

D could not profitably deviate by offering any manufacturer a P_{dj} less than $(w_{cr}-w_d)q_c$ for exclusivity. If he did, R would offer a transfer price to that manufacturer that would allow him to earn more profit than the exclusivity payment. The manufacturer would accept and D would earn zero from the competitive segment.

Finally Lemmas 1 and 2 imply that R could not benefit by deviating and offering any set of manufacturers a positive payment for exclusivity.

Uniqueness.

D would earn zero profit from the contestable segment and only $(w_d-w_{nr})q_n$ in the non-contestable segment in an equilibrium in which no exclusives were offered and R sold positive quantities. If D were to deviate and adopted the strategy in proposition 1 above, it would be individually rational for each manufacturer to accept exclusivity and not breach, and D would earn the profits outlined in proposition 1, which exceed $(w_d-w_{nr})q_n$.   *QED*

Proof of Proposition 2

Lemma 3: If $m(w_{zr}-w_d) > w_d$,

then $w_d(q_c-q_z) - m(w_{cr}-w_d)(q_c-q_z) > w_dq_c - m(w_{zr}-w_d)q_z - m(w_{cr}-w_d)(q_c-q_z)$.

Proof: Subtracting the RHS of the second equality from the LHS yields

$[m(w_{zr}-w_d) - w_d]q_z > 0$, which is true if and only if $m(w_{zr}-w_d) > w_d$.

Lemma 4: D offers each of the m manufacturers a payment of $(q_c-q_z)(w_{cr}-w_d)$ if their purchases of r are no greater than $(q_z/m)/(q_z/m + (q_c-q_z)/f + q_n/f)$ of their input purchases. Each manufacturer accepts. D offers $t_{djs} = w_d$ for all j and $s \in \{n, c\text{-}z)$ and $t_{djz} = 0$. If a manufacturer breaches the market share agreement, D will set $t_{djc} = 0$. R offers $t_{rjs} = w_{zr} - w_d$. At these prices no manufacturer breaches.

The m manufacturers offer r-based units at $w_{zr} - w_d$ to the q_z end users and offer only d-based units at w_d to the remaining end users. Each of the m manufacturers sells q_z/m r-based units and $(q_c\text{-}q_z)/f + q_n/f)$ d-based units and earns a payoff of $(q_c\text{-}q_z)(w_{cr}\text{-}w_d)$. R earns a payoff of $(w_{zr} - w_d)q_z$ and D's payoff is $w_d(q_n+q_c\text{-}q_z) - m(q_c\text{-}q_z)(w_{cr}\text{-}w_d)$.

Proof: At these prices no manufacturer has an incentive to breach. Breach would cause D to lower the price in the c segment to 0 which means the q_z r-based units could be sold for no more than $w_{zr} - w_d$ and the $q_c\text{-}q_z$ units could be sold for no more than $w_{cr} - w_d$. Thus, no breaching manufacturer could earn positive payoff from selling q_z units, and no more than $(w_{cr} - w_d)(q_c\text{-}q_z)$ from selling the $q_c - q_z$ units, which it already earns.

No manufacturer has an incentive to offer units in the non-contestable segment because any unit sold there would cause a breach of the market share agreement and the loss of the fixed payment.

R has no incentive to set different prices to induce breach. At the current prices he earns $(w_{zr} - w_d)q_z$ and each of the m manufacturers earns $(w_{cr} - w_d)(q_c\text{-}q_z)$. The maximum rent that can be earned from the c segment if D sets $t_{djc} = 0$ in case of breach is $(w_{zr} - w_d)q_z + (w_{cr} - w_d)(q_c\text{-}q_z)$. Since R would have to give a manufacturer more than $(w_{cr} - w_d)(q_c\text{-}q_z)$ to breach, he would earn less than $(w_{zr} - w_d)q_z$.   *QED*

References

Abito, Jose-Miguel, and Julian Wright. (2008), "Exclusive Dealing with Imperfect Downstream Competition." *International Journal of Industrial Organization*, 26(1): 227-46.

Aghion, Phillippe and Patrick Bolton (1987), "Contracts as a Barrier to Entry," *American Economic Review* 77, pp. 388-. 401

"Antitrust: Commission imposes fine of €1.06 bn on Intel for abuse of dominant position; orders Intel to cease illegal practices." 13/05/2009, Reference: IP/09/745 http://europa.eu/rapid/pressReleasesAction.do?reference=IP/09/745&format=HTML&aged=0&language=EN&guiLanguage=en

Bernheim, B. Douglas, and Michael Whinston. (1998), "Exclusive Dealing." *The Journal of Political Economy*, 106(1): 64-103.

Chen, Zhijun and Greg Shaffer, "Naked exclusion with minimum share requirements" (Simon School of Mgt working paper)

DeGraba, Patrick (2009) Naked Exclusion: Punishments by a Dominant Supplier for Nonexclusivity (in progress).

Doganoglu, Toker & Wright, Julian, (2010), "Exclusive dealing with network effects," *International Journal of Industrial Organization*, 28(2): 145-154.

Economides, Nicholas (2009) "Loyalty/requirement rebates and the Antitrust Modernization Commission: What is the appropriate liability standard?" *The Antitrust Bulletin* 54,(2): 259-279.

European Commission, *"EU Competition Law Update Guidance on the Commission's Enforcement Priorities in Applying Article 82 Ec Treaty to Abusive Exclusionary Conduct by Dominant Undertakings"* Brussels Dec.10, 2008

Fumagalli, Chiara, and Massimo Motta. (2006), "Exclusive Dealing and Entry, when Buyers Compete." *American Economic Review*, 96(3): 785-95.

Greenlee, Patrick, David Reitman and David S. Sibley (2008) "An antitrust analysis of bundled loyalty discounts," *International Journal of Industrial Organization* 26 (4): 1132–1152.

"In the Matter of Intel Corporation, a corporation," Docket No 9341, (August 10, 2010) http://www.ftc.gov/os/adjpro/d9341/100810intelconsent.pdf.

"In the Matter of McCormick & Company, Incorporated, a corporation," Compliant Docket No. C-3939. http://www.ftc.gov/os/2000/05/mccormickcmp.htm

In the Matter of Polypore International, Inc., a corporation. Complaint Docket No. 9327, (FTC File No. 081-0131) Sept 2008, http://www.ftc.gov/os/adjpro/d9327/091008cmp9327.pdf

Innes, Robert and Richard Sexton, (1994) Strategic Buyers and Exclusionary Contracts," *American Economic Review*, 84(3), 566-84.

Lafontaine, Francine and Margaret E. Slade, "Exclusive Contracts and Vertical Restraints Empirical Evidence and Public Policy," In P. Buccirossi ed., *Handbook of Antitrust Economics* MIT Press (2008) pp 391 – 414.

Mathewson, Frank and Ralph, Winter. (1987) "The Competitive Effects of Vertical Agreements: Comment," *American Economic Review*, 77, 1057-62.

O'Brien Daniel and Greg Shaffer, (1997) "Nonlinear Supply Contracts, Exclusive Dealing, and Equilibrium Market Foreclosure," *Journal of Economics and Management Strategy*, 6(4): 755–785.

Ordover, Janusz and Greg Shaffer, (2007) "Exclusionary Discounts," working paper

Rasmusen Eric B., J. Mark Ramseyer, and John S. Wiley, Jr. (1991), "Naked Exclusion." *American Economic Review*, 81(5): 1137-45.

Segal, Ilya R., and Michael D. Whinston. (2000), "Naked Exclusion: Comment." *American Economic Review*, 90(1): 296–309.

Settlement agreement between Advanced Micro Devices Inc. and Intel Corporation, November 11, 2009, http://download.intel.com/pressroom/legal/AMD_settlement_agreement.pdf .

Simpson, John, and Abraham L. Wickelgren. (2007 a), "Naked Exclusion, Efficient Breach, and Downstream Competition." *American Economic Review*, 97(4): 1305-20.

Simpson, John, and Abraham L. Wickelgren. (2007 b)Bundled Discounts, Leverage Theory, and Downstream Competition" *American Law and Economics Review* V9 N1: 1-14.

State of New York, by Attorney General Andrew M. Cuomo v. Intel Corporation, in the United States District Court for the District of Delaware, C.A. No. 09-827 (JJF) (2009). http://online.wsj.com/public/resources/documents/Intelcomplaint1104.pdf

Whinston, Michael **(**1990**), "**Tying, Foreclosure, and Exclusion," *American Economic Review*, 80, 837-59.

Whinston, Michael, (2006) "Chapter 4, Exclusionary Vertical Contracts," *Lectures on Antitrust Economics*. Cambridge, MA: MIT Press.

Wright, Julian, (2009) "Exclusive Dealing and Entry, when Buyers Compete: Comment," *American Economic Review*, 99(3):1070-81.